A PAGEANT OF
KINGS AND QUEENS

Henry Tudor Crowned on Bosworth Field

A Pageant of

KINGS AND QUEENS

By M. and C. E. CARRINGTON

Illustrated by
IRIS BROOKE

CAMBRIDGE
AT THE UNIVERSITY PRESS
1937

CAMBRIDGE UNIVERSITY PRESS
Cambridge, New York, Melbourne, Madrid, Cape Town,
Singapore, São Paulo, Delhi, Tokyo, Mexico City

Cambridge University Press
The Edinburgh Building, Cambridge CB2 8RU, UK

Published in the United States of America by Cambridge University Press, New York

www.cambridge.org
Information on this title: www.cambridge.org/9780521235969

First published 1937
First paperback edition 2011

A catalogue record for this publication is available from the British Library

ISBN 978-0-521-23596-9 Paperback

CONTENTS

CONTENTS

ILLUSTRATIONS

PREFACE

The continuity of our history and the long tradition of the English monarchy are the lessons to be learned in Coronation year; they form the theme of this book, which relates the triumphs and failures of English Kings and Queens, the duties they have performed at different periods of history, and the new responsibilities which have preserved the vigour of the monarchy in the present age.

When King George VI and Queen Elizabeth are crowned in Westminster Abbey the same ceremonies will be performed as were used at the Coronation of his remote ancestor Athelstan who was reigning in the year 937, a thousand years ago. The ceremonies and the regalia are here described, and an historical record is presented for young readers.

C. E. C.
M. C.
I. B.

December 1936

Chapter I

THE FIRST KINGS OF ENGLAND

THIS royal throne of kings, this sceptred isle—that is how our greatest poet has described the island of Britain. With those words he calls to mind the long procession of Kings and Queens whom our ancestors honoured in the past, as we honour our King and Queen today. From the beginning of history men have been ruled by kings —and those kings have been regarded as sacred. In heathen times, kings were held to be the ministers of the gods or were even worshipped as if they themselves were gods. When nations became Christian they regarded their kings as the servants of the one true God, and when a new king came to the throne he was "hallowed", that is, made holy, by a religious ceremony.

The first Christian king-making of which we read in these islands was the hallowing of Aidan, King of Scots, by Saint Columba in the holy island of Iona, more than thirteen hundred years ago, when the Angles and Saxons in England were still heathens. We do not know what prayers and rites were used, but we can guess that Saint Columba had in mind the many stories about the making of kings which are to be found in the Bible.

"Zadok the priest took an horn of oil out of the tabernacle, and anointed Solomon. And they blew the trumpet; and all the people said, GOD SAVE KING SOLOMON. Then Solomon sat on the throne of the Lord as king...And all the princes, and the mighty men, and all the sons likewise of king David, submitted themselves unto Solomon the king."

In that way Solomon was made king, and of other Jewish kings the Bible tells that they were invested with a mantle and a crown. When the Kings of England are crowned the old ceremonies are repeated; the king is seated on a throne, he is anointed, he is crowned, the people shout GOD SAVE THE KING, and the leaders of the people swear to be faithful to him. Also as the Anglo-Saxon Kings did, he makes a promise to rule justly.

For hundreds of years after the time of Saint Columba, Saxon tribes fought against each other and against the Welsh, until one royal family, the House of Wessex, made themselves supreme and became the first kings of England. King George VI can trace his descent through thirty-eight generations to Egbert, King of Wessex, who became overlord of all England about the year 829. Among other victories he conquered what is now the county of Surrey, and from his day Kingston-on-Thames was a royal town. There the kings of Wessex were acclaimed by the shouts of the warriors, were raised shoulder-high on a shield to be seen by the people, and were enthroned on a stone seat in the market-place. When King Egbert in his scarlet cloak, with gold bracelets on his arms, the royal helmet on his head, and a drawn sword in his hand, was lifted up by his loyal followers he was thinking perhaps of his ancestors; for like all the Saxon kings he traced his descent back to the Northern gods. If he could have seen the future he would have been prouder still, for it was his family that was to unite England, and his descendants who were to rule it for a thousand years and more.

Egbert's son succeeded him as King of Wessex and overlord of England, and after him came four grandsons of whom the youngest, Alfred, was to be so beloved in his own time that men called him "England's Darling" —so honoured ever since that he is the only one of all our kings whom we call "The Great". We are told that his father loved him more than his brothers, and when he was only four years old sent him all the way to Rome to be blessed by the Pope. It was a strange journey for so young a child, and even perilous. No doubt a guard of trusty warriors rode with him, for there would be robbers by the way as well as wolves, and jogging with pack-horses all across Europe must have taken many weary months. What a splendid city Rome must have seemed to the little boy's eyes with its churches and palaces after the wooden halls of his father and the thatched huts of Winchester. Per-

haps he carried back to England a vision of what it too might become some day. It could not have seemed likely then that he would ever be king as he had three elder brothers; but years later, when it did fall to his lot, Englishmen remembered how he had been hallowed at Rome, and no doubt their loyalty was the more freely given.

We are told that Alfred did not want to be king. He was at heart a scholar and a craftsman and would willingly have spent his life among books. And yet he was a man of action too, so that when suddenly in the midst of battle the call came to him to take up the burden of the kingship, he was able to do it magnificently. It was indeed a burden at that time, for the Danes were coming in their long ships, hundreds and thousands of them, trying to conquer the land of the Saxons for themselves. It was so terrible a time that the Saxon people were willing to forget their different kingdoms, and fight together under the kings of Wessex. Alfred's three brothers had short and bitter reigns, and when the third one died of his wounds in Wimborne Abbey, with the Danes almost at the door, it was a sword rather than a sceptre that Alfred must take up. His councillors and soldiers must have chosen him even as he stood beside his brother's body, for in Saxon times there was no regular order of succession as there is now. If the last king's son was a child or unsuitable, the nobles chose the best man from the royal family. There was no doubt now. They must have kissed his hands in homage, and raised him high for all the warriors to acclaim, and

The boy Alfred riding to Rome

as the news spread slowly through the troubled land, all men must have echoed the shout, "Long live King Alfred!"

Some say that Alfred was crowned at Winchester, but there is no record of it. There would have been little time for ceremonies in the first years of his reign, for he was fighting continually, or lying hidden in woods and marshes. There was little need either, for had he not been hallowed by the very head of the Christian Church? But in the end he won peace for his people and honour for his country, and there was time for the building of royal halls and for the dignities of rank. One thing we do know. Alfred had a crown, made for him by one of the craftsmen whom he always loved to employ. Hundreds of years later it was still treasured in England, and was described as being "of gold wire work, set with slight stones and hung with bells".

As far as we know that was the first English crown. Nowadays we are so used to the idea that it seems obvious for kings to have crowns, but it was not always so, and to find its origin we must go back to the Roman Empire which once had ruled the world. The Romans used to crown their poets and athletes with wreaths of laurel, and the emperors wore wreaths of golden leaves. These were not at first a special sign of royalty, for all the Roman heroes were crowned with leaves of some sort. Eastern kings wore an ornament called the *diadem*, a band of richly embroidered silk or linen tied round the head. Often it was studded with gems and in later times was adorned with leaves and branches of gold, like the Roman wreath.

Gradually this kind of crown came to be the special emblem of a king.

Thus we find that Charlemagne, King of the Franks, who conquered most of what is now France and Germany and much more besides and was hailed as a new emperor, had a golden crown set on his head by the Pope himself in 800. And in the same century in England the stern helmet of the Saxon kings gave place to a jewelled band of gold, wrought with a filigree of leaves. Thus ancient Rome contributed to our rite of king-making, but the little bells must have been Alfred's own fancy, for they are unique in the history of crowns.

Alfred died in the year 900, leaving a loyal kingdom to his son. It was only half of England, for he had agreed to the Danes settling in the Northern part, in order to have peace. But his children carried on his work, and forty years after his death his grandson Athelstan conquered the North and became in truth King of All England.

Chapter II

THE HOUSE OF WESSEX

IT was in 937, just a thousand years ago, that Alfred's grandson united all England. Since then the kingdom has never again been divided. The House of Wessex continued to rule it, producing many fine kings, most of whom were hallowed at Kingston-on-Thames. There is the ancient stone, still to be seen in the market-place, on which they sat in royal state to be acclaimed by their people. One of them was Edgar the Peaceful. He enjoyed such power and prosperity that after he had been king some years he had a second coronation at Bath, and again wore his crown at a great assembly at Chester, where six kings from Wales, Scotland and the islands met him and rowed him up the Dee in a barge as an act of homage.

Then came darker times for the Saxons. The Danes were harrying the coasts again, and the men of England, beaten to their knees, chose Sweyn of Denmark for their king. He was acknowledged by all the land, and his son Canute, who succeeded him, was faithfully served by Saxon thanes and proved himself worthy of their loyalty.

But the days of the Saxon kings were not quite over. When Canute and his sons were dead, the chief councillors (or Witan) chose, as king, Edward of the House of Wessex. Unlike his warrior ancestors he was meek and mild, more suited to be a monk than a king. But the Saxons, in spite of their warlike spirit, were a deeply religious race. They honoured their saintly king for his piety and cherished his memory long after his death. Edward's reign was the last gleam in the twilight of the Saxon kings. The clouds were lowering, and as soon as he was dead, the storm broke.

Somewhere about the year 1000 the Coronation Service was written down, and copies of that precious manuscript still exist. So we know just what happened on Easter Day, 1043, when Edward the Confessor was crowned in Winchester.

The church in which Edward was crowned was not one of the great cathedrals we know, and was no bigger than a parish church of today, a stone building rather

high for its length and very dark inside. We should think it very small, but the Saxons no doubt admired it greatly, and made up for the darkness by hundreds of candles and by gorgeous hangings on the altar. A carved wooden chair or wide stool would be set up as a throne, and it too would be draped with fine clothes embroidered with silver and gold.

The first part of the ceremony did not take place in the church, but in some hall nearby where the Witan elected the new king. From there two bishops led him by the hand to the church, followed by a choir of chanting monks and all the great men of the land. We may be sure it was a gorgeous procession, for there would be many other bishops and abbots all wearing robes of scarlet and blue and gold, and the nobles who followed would be in their finest array with fur-edged tunics and jewelled sword-belts. As many as possible would crowd into the church, and a great throng remain outside.

In this manner Edward was led to the altar, where he prostrated himself humbly while the *Te Deum* was sung. Then, having risen, he turned himself to the people, and the bishop called upon them to declare again whether this was their rightful king. The people answered with a great shout, which was taken up by the crowd outside. This ceremony, which ensures against anyone's taking the king's place at the last moment, is called the Recognition and is still part of our Coronation. After that, Edward repeated the same promise that the kings of earlier days had made, that he would preserve peace in the Church and throughout the land, and that he would rule with justice and mercy. This is called the Oath, and something very similar has been promised by every one of our kings.

Next the actual hallowing took place. While the choir sang, as an anthem, the account of Solomon's coronation, quoted on the second page of this book, the holy oil was poured upon Edward's head with a prayer of blessing. Now he was king, and ready to receive the *regalia* or signs of royalty. First he was dressed in robes which were something like those of a bishop to show the religious nature of his office. In the quaint pictures of the time we see him in a long white tunic, with another embroidered one over it, and a gorgeous cloak (or pall).

Then with more prayers a ring was put on his finger and a sword girded to his side, and with the words "God crown thee with a crown of glory", the bishop set the crown upon his head. The sceptre was put into his right hand and the rod into his left, and there he sat upon the throne in all his royal state.

There followed a long blessing and lastly this prayer: "Bless, O Lord, the Virtuous Carriage of this King, and accept the work of his hands; replenish his realm with the blessing of Heaven, of the dew of the water and of the deeps. Let the influence of the sun and moon drop fatness upon the high mountains, and the clouds plenty upon the low valleys, that the earth may abound with the store of all things: The Lord that sitteth in Heaven be his defender for ever and ever for Jesus Christ our Lord." After this the Mass was celebrated and the ceremony was over.

This order of service became the model for future coronations not only in England, but in the principal countries of Europe, France and Italy in particular having copied it almost word for word. In England it has been revised several times and new details added, but its main features are still the same, and even the words of the prayers have suffered little change (except that of being translated from Latin into English at the Reformation). The anthem at the anointing, the words at the moment of crowning and the last prayer are examples of the ancient words which are still in use.

St Edward (as he was afterwards called) was not crowned with Alfred's crown. A new and more magnificent one was made for him, ornamented with alternate crosses and lilies and studded with precious stones. This crown and all his regalia were used for the coronations of all our kings down to Charles I. What became of them then you will hear later. In 1450 a monk of Westminster made a list of them as follows:

"St Edward, King and Confessor, for the memory of posterity and the dignity of the royal coronation, caused to be preserved in this church all the royal ornaments with which he was crowned: namely his tunic, overtunic, bracelets, girdle and embroidered pall (cloak); a pair of buskins (shoes), a pair of gloves, a golden sceptre, one wooden rod gilt, another of iron.

"Also an excellent crown, a golden comb and a spoon.

"Also for the coronation of the queen a crown and two rods.

"Also for the communion of the Lord King...one

Saint Edward the Confessor

chalice of onyx stone...and a paten of the best gold. All of which are to be considered precious relics."

It is a little difficult to see what all the sceptres and rods are for. They are very ancient symbols of power, and in old pictures the king generally has one with a golden dove on it in one hand and one with a cross in the other. The spoon was to pour the oil and the comb to arrange his hair afterwards.

St Edward's ring, which was called "The wedding ring of England", had a great sapphire in it. There is a legend that in his usual generosity he gave it to a poor beggar, who appeared again years after and disclosed himself as John the Baptist, giving back the ring. After that it was set in the crown. It is the only relic of St Edward that we still have, for after many adventures it has found again its place of honour in the crown.

By this time London was beginning to grow into an important city, with a constant coming and going of ships to its wharves. King Edward made it his chief resort rather than the older capital of Winchester, and it became his great ambition to found near it an abbey where the sacred regalia might be cherished, and where monks might chant for ever to the glory of God. The old town of London, that part which we now call the City, was huddled within its walls, and further upstream on an island in the marshes stood a wooden church, which, according to the legend, had been blessed by St Peter, in the guise of a fisherman. This church the king resolved to rebuild, and, gathering about him learned monks and skilled French craftsmen, he devoted himself to raising the finest church that England had ever seen. He was an old white-haired man before it was done. On Innocents' Day (28 December), 1065, it was consecrated, and eight days later on Twelfth Night he died. Next day he was buried above the high altar, where his body still lies.

Then came the storm. The Danes were on the war-path yet again, and the Duke of Normandy had cast covetous eyes on England. The last heirs left to the royal house of Wessex were two children, Edward's nephew and niece, so the Witan chose Harold, the young brother of the queen and a tried soldier. He was crowned in haste in the new abbey, and he then marched with his army north to defeat the Danes—then south to Hastings. How he fell on that fatal field is the best known event in our history. On that dark day, 14 October 1066, the whole Saxon army was broken, and Duke William, riding among his mailed knights, was master of England.

Some bold spirits stood out against this fate, paying for it dearly, others fled the land, but the greater part of the Saxon people bowed their heads unwillingly to what could not be avoided. The powerless Witan elected William king, and on Christmas Day Archbishop Aldred with a heavy heart set St Edward's crown upon the Conqueror's head.

Chapter III

THE AGE OF CHIVALRY

KING William was a mighty warrior and hunter, harsh to those who crossed his path, but just to all who served him well. He had conquered England by his own energy, and he founded a line of kings who held it so strongly that it never was conquered again. Many of his characteristics can be seen in the Norman and Plantagenet kings who followed him. Some had his big build and great strength, some his iron will, while others were merely obstinate. Nearly all inherited his hot temper and his personal bravery. But as we follow the long procession of them through the centuries the interesting thing is how they began as foreign conquerors whose interests, customs and language were French, and how after a few generations they became English kings and proud to be so.

A striking example of how the customs of Old England survived the Conquest is the Coronation Service. The haughty William submitted to every point of the Saxon ceremony and was crowned with exactly the same ritual as St Edward and Harold. The Chronicle tells us how "Archbishop Aldred hallowed him to king at Westminster and also swore him ere he would set the crown on his head, that he would so well govern this nation as any king before him best did, if they would be faithful unto him." The Norman soldiers, waiting outside the abbey, did not know the customs of the Saxon ceremony, and when they heard the shout go up at the Recognition they thought there must be a riot going on inside. So they turned on any unfortunate Saxons who had joined the crowd and were cutting them down with their swords and setting fire to their houses, when William himself, hearing the commotion, left his throne and strode down the aisle. His appearance at the door, crowned and robed, was enough to quell his turbulent followers.

William had wasted little time or money over this ceremony, and as soon as it was over he set about enforcing his rule over the land. When the old landowners defied him he simply took all their lands and gave them to his barons to keep and rule. In return they had to swear to be his true men and fight for him when called on. English thanes could only keep their lands by taking the same oath. Sometimes they were bound to perform some more personal duty to the king instead of the military service, or as a little extra to remind them from time to time that they were his servants. It might be to give him a red rose on May Day or some such fanciful act of homage, or it might be to carry his sword on state occasions or wait on him at table. They had held their lands in the same way in Normandy, and regarded these duties as honours rather than as acts of servitude.

When England was sufficiently subdued, William sent for his wife Matilda to come from Normandy with their children and be crowned Queen of England. And in order to make the occasion more impressive he chose to be crowned again with her. During the ceremonies of the day, the barons performed their duties for their new lands, and so did English thanes who wanted to keep their old ones. One was called "Marshall". He arranged the processions, and kept order, pressing back unruly crowds with his staff or baton. Others carried the regalia of the king and queen, and many acted as servants at the great banquet that followed. There was the "Chief Butler", who passed the king his goblet of wine, and the "Grand Panneter", who served him with bread and carried in the knives and salt-cellars. The king's favourite cook had been given the manor of Addington, and his task was to make and present a dish of "dilligrout" (a kind of white soup which William liked), a duty which his heirs faithfully performed for seven hundred years. Each was given a fee for his service. The Butler had the king's goblet, while the Panneter could keep the salt-cellars.

In the middle of the banquet a fully armed knight on horseback clattered into the hall. This was the Lord of Marmion, whose family had held lands in Normandy for many generations for the service of acting as the king's champion. Flinging down his glove he offered to fight in single combat any man who denied that William and Matilda were the rightful king and queen. This was a new custom to England, but one that had come to stay a very long time.

For twenty years William ruled with iron severity, and the English people reconciled themselves sadly to the idea of Norman kings. This was made no easier for them by Red-Haired William II, who succeeded when his father died in Normandy. He was as bad a king as any we have had, and when he was killed by an arrow in the New Forest nobody was sorry. As he had never married, his heir was his brother Henry, who had been born in England and could even understand its language. He began his reign by the most popular marriage that ever a king has made, for he took as wife a daughter of the old royal house of Wessex. When St Edward died the only members of his family left were the grandchildren of his brother, and they, when the Normans landed, fled with their mother in a ship. After terrible storms they landed in the Firth of Forth, where the young King of Scotland, who was hunting by the sea-shore, saw them and fell instantly in love with the elder girl, later to be known as Saint Margaret because of her goodness and piety. He entertained them all in his castle, and although Margaret was a penniless outcast he insisted on marrying her. Three of their sons in succession became kings of Scotland, and it was their daughter Matilda whom Henry I married amid the great rejoicings of his people.

Henry was a wise ruler and his people were more contented, but a great tragedy was to befall him. His son, Prince William, was returning from a visit to Normandy, when the White Ship, which was carrying the young heir of England, struck a rock in mid-channel and, being over-crowded with gay young courtiers, sank instantly. For three days no one dared tell the king that his son was drowned. When at last he heard it he fell

The White Ship

unconscious to the ground and it is said that he never smiled again. So perished the prince on whom the nation had set its hope, for he was descended from Alfred as well as from the Conqueror. The only surviving person in whom those two royal lines were united was his sister Maud, but the barons would not have her as queen. The idea of a woman ruler seemed absurd to them (even her supporters gave her no higher title than "the Lady of England"), but, after long wars between her and her cousin Stephen, they agreed that her son should succeed to the throne. So through her the descendants of Alfred did sit upon the throne again.

Maud's son, Henry II (who was called Plantagenet from the sprig of broom he wore in his cap), was more of a foreigner than ever. His father was the Count of Anjou, his wife the heiress of Aquitaine, and through his mother he inherited England and Normandy. His possessions were enormous, but he had the energy of his great-grandfather, the Conqueror, and hurrying from place to place with an army, he managed to put everything in order, and even made Ireland submit to him.

Then came his son, Richard of the Lion Heart. To men of his own age he was the model of a perfect knight, for he was strong in battle, truthful and fearless, and besides, he looked magnificent on a horse. But we do not think of him as a good king, for he sacrificed England to his love of adventure and romance, draining it of money to equip his ships and armies to fight the Turks. No sooner was he crowned than away he went to try and win back Jerusalem. St George who killed the dragon was his patron saint, and on his shield he bore St George's scarlet cross. One of his galleys carried his betrothed lady, Berengaria of Navarre, for every romantic knight must fight for a lady. After many adventures he captured the island of Cyprus. "There", says a chronicler, "in the joyous month of May 1191, did King Richard solemnly take to wife his beloved lady. ...A satin tunic of rose-colour was belted round his

waist; his mantle was of striped silver tissue brocaded with half moons; his sword of fine damascus steel had a hilt of gold and a silver scaled sheath....In this attire Richard who had yellow curls and a figure like Mars himself appeared a perfect model of military and manly grace."

After the marriage Berengaria was crowned Queen of Cyprus and England. Nothing could have been more removed from the realities of English life, than this fanciful ceremony on a Grecian isle, but it was typical of

Berengaria's reign, for in all her life she never set foot in England.

No sooner was Richard home from his adventures with the Turks, than off he went again to fight the King of France. One of his favourite battle cries was "Dieu et mon droit" (God and my rights), which later became the motto in the royal arms. His feats of valour were the theme of every ballad, but one day a French archer, aiming well from his tower of defence, mortally wounded the soldier king, and the realm he had cared for so little passed to his brother John.

John was the black sheep of the family. By right he should never have been king at all, for his elder brother Geoffrey, now dead, had left a son. He was twelve years old and had been called Arthur after the heroic king of the old legends that the minstrels loved to sing. He should have been Arthur I of England, but his uncle John got him into his clutches and he was never seen again. No one knows what became of this unfortunate little prince, but the guilt of his death lies clearly on his uncle.

John quarrelled so violently with the barons that, while he was doing it, the King of France won back all Normandy and even invaded England itself.

The loss of Normandy did England no harm, for the sooner our kings gave up wasting their energies across the channel, the better it was for England. But in 1216 it seemed a judgment, as if "Heaven itself did frown upon the land".

The barons were so tired of John's rule that they offered the crown to the French king's son, but fortunately, just then, John when crossing the Wash one cold night after eating too much for dinner caught a fever and died. Then the barons were quite ready to have his young son Henry as king, and they quickly drove the French out of the country.

The prince on whom the English set their hope, John's nine-year-old son, Henry III, was the first child king since the Conquest.

Chapter IV

SOLDIER KINGS

THE children of King John were in Gloucester with their mother when the news came that he was dead, and at once she had Henry proclaimed king in the streets. Nine days later he was crowned in Gloucester Cathedral with one of her golden "throat collars". It is often said that this was because John had lost the crown of England, when all his baggage sank in the quicksands of the Wash. He certainly did lose his crown on that fateful night, but the kings of the Middle Ages wore crowns every day, and they each had several as part of their wardrobe. At the least they would have a light circlet for general wear, and that was what John lost. The crown of St Edward, which was used for coronations and for nothing else, was in safe keeping at Westminster; Henry could not be crowned with it because the King of France held London. After these troubles had blown over, Henry was crowned again at Westminster with the proper regalia.

When Henry married Eleanor of Provence, her coronation and the banquet after it provided the most gorgeous spectacle that England had yet seen. There are detailed accounts of this gay occasion, and we find in them that the barons were all quarrelling over their rights to perform services to the King and Queen. Citizens of certain royal towns also had duties, which they considered honours, and Matthew Paris, a monk who was present, writes:

"On the same day they (the citizens of London) set out from the city for Westminster, to perform the duties of butler to the king at the coronation, which office belongs to them by ancient right. They proceeded thither dressed in rich garments, with mantles of cloth of gold and handsome tippets; they were mounted on rich steeds and arrayed in troops in order. They carried 360 cups of gold or silver, and the royal trumpeters went in front of them sounding their trumpets; so remarkable a novelty struck all who beheld it with astonishment.... The Wardens of the Cinque Ports carried a canopy above the king on four spears, this duty however was not undisputed. The Earl of Leicester supplied the king with water in a basin to wash before dining. The Justiciar of the Forests arranged the dishes on the king's right hand, although that first met with some opposition. The citizens of London passed the wine about in costly cups, and those of Winchester superintended the cooking of the feast."

Unfortunately Henry III was much too fond of spending his money on feasts, and although he reigned a long time he never learned to rule well. But he did complete one magnificent work, the rebuilding of Westminster Abbey in its present form, on the foundations of the Confessor's church. Since then it has been a worthy scene of royal pageants, the burial-place of most of our kings, and one of the glories of England. Henry had a beautiful shrine built over the tomb of St Edward and called his eldest son after him, bringing back the good old Saxon name to our royal line.

Edward I was away on a crusade when his father died, but he hurried back with his devoted Queen Eleanor, and was received with great joy in London. At the coronation banquet, which was more splendid than ever, the King of Scotland came and knelt in homage—then to show the generous spirit of the occasion he and many of the barons let loose their horses with all their costly trappings, shouting to the eager crowds who thronged round the hall, that whoever caught them could keep them.

Alexander of Scotland had done homage, but not Llewelyn of Wales. Since the coming of the Normans the Welsh princes had admitted more or less unwillingly that the kings of England were their overlords, and Edward was not the man to allow any backslidings now. He led an army into Wales, and after several campaigns in the mountains defeated Prince Llewelyn who was killed in battle. He told the Welsh chieftains, who were clamouring to keep their own country under a Welsh prince, that he would give them a prince who was born in Wales and could not speak a word of English. When they were waiting anxiously to see who it would be, he appeared holding in his arms his little new-born son. Since then the eldest son of every king has been made Prince of Wales. But the first baby prince was not the

The First Prince of Wales

eldest. He had an elder brother Alphonso, who had been with his father on the campaign, and had ridden to London to offer the captured coronet of Wales at the shrine of St Edward. This promising prince died young, so his name, chosen by his Spanish mother, never was the name of an English king.

Edward I would have liked to add Scotland also to the royal titles of England, and when King Alexander died leaving only a little girl in Norway as heir, he set about arranging that she should marry his son. But the poor "Maid of Norway" had such a rough crossing to her new kingdom that she died of the effects. So Edward had to find another way of getting Scotland into his power. He soon made an excuse to march into it with a great army, but although he was as fine a soldier as any of his forefathers, he could not conquer the Scottish people. After many bloody battles he made a treaty and came away, bringing with him one of the most treasured possessions of Scotland, the sacred Stone of Scone. Legend said that this was the very stone on which Jacob had pillowed his head when he saw the vision of the angels, and that it had been brought to Ireland and thence to Scotland by heroes of the past. Probably it had always been at Scone, but as far as history goes back the kings of Scotland were always hallowed upon it.

Edward had it set in a fine chair and meant that his descendants should be crowned upon it for evermore. So they have been, but he did not foresee that, though the stone was never returned to Scone, the Scottish kings came to London instead. For in 1603 (three hundred years after Edward I) the King of Scotland inherited the crown of England, and since then the monarch of both countries is crowned on the sacred stone. It stands in St Edward's Chapel in the abbey, and is sometimes, wrongly, called St Edward's chair.

Edward I was a great king who made good laws. Among other things for which he is remembered are the crosses he set up in memory of his Queen Eleanor, whom he loved so much. When she died at Grantham, he followed her funeral procession sorrowfully all the way to Westminster, and ordered a stone cross to be built at every spot where her bier rested for the night. Charing Cross was the last of these.

But the son of this devoted couple did not take after them. In spite of his fine start (as first Prince of Wales) and his good old name, he was a failure as a king. Even at his coronation things went wrong, for he entrusted the arrangements to his favourite Piers Gaveston, who offended the barons by denying them their old privileges. Gaveston was not even efficient, and the banquet was extremely late.

This reign that had begun badly had a worse end, for Edward II was deposed and murdered.

The next Edward was only a boy at his father's death,

but as soon as he began to grow up it was clear that he took after his grandfather. He was a keen soldier and was all afire to go to war with someone and win new honours for himself and England. The King of France had just died, and as Edward's mother was a French princess he put forward his claim to the title. When this was ignored he simply assumed it. From that time every monarch of England styled himself King of France, until in 1801 George III agreed to drop the absurdity.

But Edward III was not content with titles, he collected an army and launched the French war that was to last a hundred years. No sooner had he left England than the Scots invaded it, but his queen, Philippa, herself led an army northwards, which defeated them and brought back young King David of Scotland as a prisoner. After that she hastened to join the king in Normandy. This warlike pair had a fine family of strapping sons. The eldest (another Edward), generally known as the Black Prince, was the pride of England for his courage and courtesy. For his valour at Crécy he was knighted on the battlefield, and afterwards won a great victory of his own at Poitiers. The King of France himself was brought back to London as a prisoner, and it is often told how the prince, instead of showing pride at his triumph, acted as his squire with the humility of a true knight, waiting on him at table and offering him his cup on bended knee. The Black Prince took as his motto the German phrase, "Ich Dien", which means "I serve", the motto of every succeeding Prince of Wales.

That winter, 1358, there were two prisoner kings in

London and great feasts were held in their honour with tournaments and revelry. The Black Prince was the hero of it all, but another blow was in store for England, for he died just before his father, and the crown passed to his little son, nine-year-old Richard of Bordeaux.

Chapter V

A FOURTEENTH-CENTURY CORONATION

S O the pageant of history goes on, and all this time the regalia of kings was treasured at Westminster by monks and abbots, while the sacred ceremonies of coronation were guarded just as jealously against all change. In each generation the barons claimed their rights to do just what their forefathers had done, and the bishops saw to it that not one prayer or blessing was left out.

From Edward the Confessor to Edward III the only changes were additions. During those three hundred years men's way of life became more civilized, and their wealth greater. These things were reflected in the Coronation Service, enriching it with new details, until in the fourteenth century it reached its most splendid form. Since then another six hundred years have passed, but little more has been added and little has been left out. Although the service we use now is in its main framework as old as England itself, its details and pageantry belong to the days when Edward III and the Black Prince led their armies to war with trumpets blowing, banners flying and all the knights of England ready to die for honour's sake.

The Coronation is a ceremony of the Age of Chivalry, and Chivalry means Knighthood. The knight was the hero of the age and all good men cultivated the knightly virtues of courage and loyalty and courtesy. But knighthood was not for everyone; it was very rarely conferred upon those who were not nobly born. When a young squire had proved his worth, he took a vow to be true to God and the king, and was then tapped on the shoulder with a sword and invested with golden spurs, the badge of his new rank. King's sons were knighted very young; the Black Prince was only fifteen when he won his spurs in battle at Crécy.

Some knights were banded together in societies for a special object. The Templars were knights sworn to defend the Temple at Jerusalem, the Hospitallers or Knights of St John protected pilgrims on their way to the Holy Land, the Teutonic Knights fought against the heathen in Prussia. But other Orders of Knights were bound in comradeship merely by a special oath and a badge. On the day before the coronation the king chose certain young squires, who were bathed and dressed in splendid robes as a sign of undertaking a new way of life, with pure hearts. Then they were knighted and known as the Knights of the Bath. Edward III founded the most famous of all orders, the Knights of the Garter, who wore as a badge a jewelled garter below the left knee, and as a robe a cloak of blue velvet.

In battle, when knights were covered head to foot in armour, they wore a crest on their helmets and a device on their shields, so that they could be recognized. This was the beginning of the curious art of Heraldry, which was a serious matter when few people could read or write. Everyone could recognize the Star of De Vere, the Portcullis of the Beauforts, the Bear-and-Ragged-Staff of Warwick, the Leopards of England, and the Lilies of France. The pattern on a knight's shield became the badge of his family and was used by his relations with some slight "difference". If he married into a noble family his wife's shield might be placed beside his own; if he performed a famous deed it would be recorded by a new addition to his coat-of-arms. When Edward III claimed the throne of France he "quartered" the French lilies with the English leopards (or lions) in the royal arms, and there they remained for five hundred years.

Servants wore the badge of their lord embroidered on their coats, and the king's heralds, whom he used as messengers and for making royal proclamations, were richly clad in coats bearing the arms of England. Each great earl kept his herald, and the king had heralds for each of the provinces of his realm, and heralds for each of the orders of knighthood. They bore, and still bear, strange titles—Bluemantle was an officer of the Knights of the Garter; Norroy was herald of the northern kingdom, England north of Trent; Lancaster herald for the Duchy of Lancaster. The chief herald was called a King-at-Arms; his person was sacred like that of the king, for whom he spoke, and he wore a coronet. Richard III founded the College of Heralds, making rules for their offices, and giving them the right to determine what were the proper coats-of-arms for different families to bear.

When Edward III died, the coronation of his grandson, Richard, was celebrated with the utmost pomp of heraldry and chivalry.

The full order of service is preserved in the *Liber Regalis* (or Royal Book). This is how Richard II was made king.

First he was proclaimed by the heralds (just as George VI was proclaimed in 1936). Then the Court of Claims met under the presidency of Richard's eldest uncle, John of Gaunt, Duke of Lancaster. He claimed for himself the office of Steward, and to him all the other nobles addressed their claims to perform services to the king. He settled what everybody was to do, so that there should be no unseemly wrangling on the great day itself, and as the report of this court is still in existence we know who carried out each detail of the ceremony.

Meanwhile in the abbey "a stage" or square platform was made in the middle of the choir on which was set "a lofty throne with silken coverings". There was also a "chair of repose" prepared for the king on the south side of the chancel, and the coronation chair itself before the altar.

On the day before the coronation Richard rode bareheaded through the crowded streets of Old London to his palace at Westminster, where the Abbot of Westminster was in attendance to instruct him and pray with him before he went to bed.

In the morning all the nobles gathered in the great hall, where Richard came "being clothed with spotless apparel

and shod only with socks". (It is directed in the *Liber
Regalis* that his shirt should have various openings which
could be closed with silver loops, so that he could be
anointed in several places.) Over his white clothes he
wore an ermine cloak and a red velvet cap, called "a cap
of estate". Seated on a throne, he awaited the arrival of
the bishops and monks of Westminster, who came from
the abbey in solemn procession bringing the regalia.
This now included far more than St Edward's relics.
Besides the crown, sceptre and robes, there were golden
sandals, a stole like a priest's, the spurs of a knight and
no less than three swords. The chief of these had a blunt
end as a sign of mercy, and was called Curtana. These
things were delivered, each one to the lord who had
the right of carrying it. Then the procession re-formed,
passing slowly over a cloth spread on the ground all the
way to the abbey. All London was elbowing to see the
show. First went the monks chanting an anthem; then
the bishops in copes and mitres; then the nobles in
gorgeous clothes, each bearing high his honourable
burden of sword or sceptre or golden spurs—royal dukes,
the king's haughty uncles—or earls, the flower of
England's knighthood; at last the boy king walking
unshod under a huge purple canopy held up by the
Barons of the Cinque Ports, with a bishop on either side.

So they came into the abbey, and passed into the choir,
where Richard mounted on to the stage, and the archbishop presented him to the people at each of its four
corners for Recognition. Each time a shout of approval
went up.

Next Richard was led to the altar, where he offered to the abbey a pound of gold and a rich pall, after which he prostrated himself on cushions before the altar, and then went to the "chair of repose", where he heard "a short and appropriate sermon".

After the sermon the Oath was read, and Richard, repeating it aloud, swore "upon the altar in sight of all" that he would keep it truly.

Then followed the Litany. After that Richard came to the great chair before the altar. His robe was removed, the loops in his shirt undone, and with the canopy of state held over him, he was anointed on the head, the hands, the breast, the back, the shoulders and elbows. When his shirt was closed again the nobles drew near, each ready to hand to the archbishop the ornament he held, while it was the chamberlain's task to help to put them on. Slowly with prayers and anthems he was arrayed—first with the white tunic, then the overtunic "reaching to his feet wrought with golden figures before and behind", buskins and spurs, belt and sword, the stole round his neck, the royal mantle, "worked all over with golden eagles", and as a grand climax the crown and ring.

The next ceremony was the offering of the sword to God. Richard (guided by the Abbot of Westminster) took the sword with which he had been girded and laid it on the altar. Immediately it was the task of "the greatest earl present" to offer its price instead (a hundred shillings), thus redeeming the sword for the king to use as God's weapon. The earl carried it before him for the rest of the day.

This done, the sceptre and rod were delivered, and the king "thus crowned and vested" kissed the bishops. Then he was led back to the stage, where all the peers of the realm stood round him, some lifting him up on to the throne (a relic of the Saxon ceremony of raising on a shield), others "stretching forth their hands...and offering to support him". One by one they took the oath of homage, and the *Liber Regalis* directs that "those who are near shall lessen the king's labour in supporting the crown, sceptre and rod".

The crown of St Edward, which had been often enriched with more jewels, was indeed far beyond young Richard's strength. Two hundred years earlier, at the crowning of the first Richard, one of the strongest men of his age, we find that two earls were appointed to hold it up on his head on "account of its weight". To a boy of eleven even the heavy robes must have been wearisome, as he sat through the long hour and more, while the homage went on. After that Mass was celebrated. Then at last Richard was relieved of his burdens, for it was the custom of the king to retire into St Edward's chapel, behind the high altar, where the chamberlain reverently took off the regalia. He was dressed again in clothes which though very splendid were more convenient, and a lighter crown was put on his head. Even then, Richard, who had eaten nothing that day (for kings were always crowned fasting), was faint with weariness, and when the grand procession returned to Westminster Hall, the new-made king was carried by two stalwart soldiers.

So he went "to his private chamber and rested there

Richard II at the Coronation Banquet

awhile, and then came down into the hall, and after washing his hands he sat in his royal seat at the high table". Then we read how once again the old families did the honours of the feast. The Duke of Norfolk was Marshal (as the present Duke is now). His duty was to "allay tumults" and to usher in the dishes to the king's table, with the Constable, both "mounted on noble chargers". The Constable was Richard's uncle John of

Gaunt, who, as first nobleman in the land, had more duties than he could perform himself. One had been to redeem the sword at the altar and carry it afterwards. This honour he gave to his young son Henry (then Earl of Derby). The Earl of Arundel was Chief Butler. Thomas Beauchamp of Warwick "served with salt-sellars and knives". Sir Thomas Blount held the king's napkin, on behalf of John de Hastings, who could not be present ("his office is of old to serve with napkins"). The Knight of Addington presented his dish of "dilligrout", and Sir John Dymoke (who had inherited the lands of the Marmions, champions to the Conqueror) rode in shining armour into the hall and gave the old challenge, which of course was not taken up.

"And all this time the said Earl of Derby, standing at the right hand of the king as he sat at table, held in his hand the said principal sword, naked and drawn."

Years after, when men looked back on these things, this last service must have seemed like an omen, for it was Henry of Derby, afterwards of Lancaster, who drew the sword of rebellion against the unfortunate Richard, did him to death, and took the crown of England for himself.

But no one thought of such things on that day of festival (St Swithun's Day, 1377). "The nobles, knights and other well-born gentlemen spent the rest of that day in dancing, leaping, and solemn minstrelsy, for joy at the solemnity. And after dinner the lord king wearied with extreme toil sought rest and sleep."

Chapter VI

FIGHTING FOR THE CROWN

NOT all the water in the rough rude sea
Can wash the balm from an anointed king.

That was what Richard thought when he grew up. His idea of his own holiness was enormous. He thought it gave him the right to do just what he liked, forgetting that his hallowing was not a one-sided affair, but a bargain in which he had promised to rule justly. There are some things for which we can like him; his love of music and all the fine arts (it was he who rebuilt Westminster Hall as it is today); and his devotion to his young wife, Anne of Bohemia. When she died he was heart-broken, and though he did marry again it was only because he wanted to have a French alliance. Isabella of France was only seven years old when she came to England to marry Richard and be crowned queen, but he received her with every honour and was always a kind and amusing playmate. The barons despised him because he allied himself with the French, instead of fighting them as his grandfather did. We admire him for preferring peace to war. But he was not a just ruler. He was not even wise, for he let his worst injustice fall

on his cousin Henry, who was one of the nearest heirs
to the throne, an ambitious man and a good soldier. So
Henry raised an army against his king, and took him
prisoner. Shakespeare, who has told Richard's sad
history, makes him cry:

> I'll give my jewels for a set of beads,
> My gorgeous palace for a hermitage
> And my large kingdom for a little grave.

The grave was all he got, for when Henry had forced
Richard to give him the crown with his own hands in
Westminster Hall, he sent him a prisoner to Pontefract
Castle, and there had him murdered.

Henry had a still more magnificent coronation in order
to make up for his doubtful claim to the throne. He was
anointed with very special oil, from a golden vessel
shaped like an eagle. It had been found hidden in the
church at Poitiers and the Black Prince had brought it
back to England as a holy relic. A tale was told that
the Virgin Mary had given the eagle with the oil to
St Thomas à Becket in a vision, telling him that it was
for anointing the true kings of England. (This eagle,
which is called the ampulla, was the only piece of the
regalia to escape destruction by Cromwell.)

In spite of this Henry IV was not a great king. It took
most of his energy to crush those who denied his right
to the throne, and he had money troubles too. He wanted
Richard II's widow, the Queen Dowager (who was now
twelve), to marry his son, handsome Prince Hal, for she
had a rich dowry, but she staunchly refused to have
anything to do with him. So he packed her off to France

and kept her money. That of course started off the quarrel with France again. Henry soon died, quite worn out. Shakespeare put into his mouth the much-quoted words: "Uneasy lies the head that wears a crown."

We may not care for Henry IV much, but his son is a more attractive figure, first as gay Prince Hal, at once the delight and terror of the London taverns for his merry ways and mad pranks, then as Henry V, the king who loved honour above all things. He had the old idea that the way to win honour was to fight the French. It was a stupid idea, for it wasted good English lives, and French ones too, and what we won we never could keep. It was a bee that buzzed in the bonnets of the English kings for three hundred years, and those who were free from it (like Henry III and Richard II) were despised as weaklings. But Henry V only thought what most men of his time heartily agreed with, and he lost no time in putting it into action with a vigour that set "all the youth of England" on fire. So once again English warhorses thundered over French fields, and the battle cry went up: "God for England, Harry, and St George."

Then came a day when Henry seemed doomed. With a little band of tired soldiers, he came face to face with more than five times as many French, fresh and confident. When his captains wished despairingly for more men, his reply was, "the fewer men, the greater share of honour", and inspired by his courage his men inflicted a crushing defeat on the great French army. As he fought in the thick of the battle on that famous field of Agincourt Henry wore, as was his custom, a crown upon his helmet, in which was set a great ruby that had been given to the Black Prince by Don Pedro of Castille. That same ruby is now the central jewel in the crown of George VI.

The knights of France lay dead in their thousands, and those who had survived were divided among themselves, for their king was old, and mad into the bargain, and they had no one to unite them. So France was Henry's for the taking, and soon he was able to dictate his terms. He was to marry the French princess, Katherine, the younger sister of Richard II's little queen, Isabella, and he was to succeed to the throne of France when her father, the mad king, was dead.

It was a triumphant hour for England. Bells pealed, and fountains ran with wine. In Paris the marriage was celebrated with the greatest pomp, and then Henry brought home his bride to be crowned. London went mad with joy, for Henry seemed god-like, and Katherine was a beauty and much in love with her hero husband although he had conquered her own people. The rejoicings broke out again when a son was born at Windsor, and called after his father; but all was turned to blank despair when that father, whom no one could conquer in battle, died of fever before the year was out.

When the old King of France died, the united crowns of England and France passed to an eight-months-old baby.

> Henry born at Monmouth
> Shall small time reign, and much get,
> But Henry of Windsor shall long reign and lose all.

This old saying was repeated in the taverns and round firesides, and men shook their heads over the prospects of the baby king. It was said that Henry V himself had thought it unlucky for his son to be born at Windsor. Time was to prove the rhyme terribly true. But for a few years all seemed fair enough. The widowed queen brought the king to London to open Parliament. Seated on her lap on a moving throne, he was drawn by white horses to Westminster, among admiring crowds. There, enthroned still on her knee, in the great hall, he happily clutched the sceptre, an attractive plaything, while the Lord Chancellor made a speech on behalf of His Majesty (who was not a year old).

To simplify the Coronation Service was thought sacrilege in the fifteenth century, but to make a baby go through it all with proper dignity seemed equally out of the question, so it was not till Henry VI was nearly eight years old that the great ceremony took place. Even then he was the youngest monarch to be crowned in England. A year later, in the great cathedral of Notre Dame in Paris, he was crowned again as King of France. The

French ceremony was almost the same as our own. Like us they had a set of holy regalia used for all coronations, and just as we dated ours from our saintly King Edward, they honoured theirs as having belonged to the Emperor Charlemagne. So the crown of Charlemagne was set on the head of young Henry, and at his side was girded the enormous sword called "Joyous" which the warrior king had wielded in battle.

It was a long and brilliant ceremony, but a hollow one, for already something very wonderful had happened. A peasant girl called Joan had led armies into battle and defeated the English again and again, inspiring her people with a faith and patriotism which they never had before. Even to the Dauphin, the son of the old mad king, she had given courage, and urged by her, he had been crowned as King of France in defiance of the English. The regalia of his ancestors was in the hands of his enemies, all except the ampulla of oil which had been used for anointing all the kings of France. In the beautiful cathedral at Rheims, the Dauphin had been anointed, while Joan, Maid of France, had stood in shining armour at his side holding high his banner. When the makeshift crown was set on his head the people had shouted "Noel! Noel!" (a word which hailed the birth of something new—Christ's birth at Christmas—or the birth of a new reign). This was the real King of France, and when the pompous coronation of Henry took place a year later, his kingdom was already half lost.

So it happened that the widowed Queen Katherine had her brother and her son crowned as rival kings of

The Baby King, Henry VI

France within a year. She had quite settled down north of the channel and had married a Welshman, Owen Tudor, as her second husband.

The English soldiers captured Joan and burned her for a witch but, under the banner which she had carried, the French drove us steadily back, until of all our conquests nothing was left but the town of Calais.

Henry VI grew into a gentle scholarly man who founded schools and colleges (Eton, for instance) and gave his money to the poor. But this was no time for a saint to wear the crown. The hot-headed, hard-fisted barons, chafing at the loss of France, needed a stern ruler, not a kindly king who forgave his enemies and was inclined to be weak in the head (for he had inherited a touch of insanity from his French grandfather). Many of the barons were of royal blood, descendants of Edward III's large family. They remembered how Henry IV had seized the crown by no better right than being the king's cousin and a stronger man. By the same right now, Henry VI's cousins drew their swords against him, and England was plunged into the "Wars of the Roses".

Many of our kings have been unfortunate. None is such a helpless and pathetic figure as Henry VI. We see him now a fugitive—now a prisoner in the Tower—now wringing his hands on a battlefield, while his queen led armies on his behalf, with her young son Edward, Prince of Wales, riding gallantly beside her.

Henry was murdered and so was his son (no great wonder in those cruel times), and with them ended the direct line of the House of Lancaster. The crime of Henry IV was avenged by another very like it, and the Duke of York reigned as Edward IV. He managed to hold the throne for his lifetime and died in his bed (no small achievement in those days). It was his two little sons who had to pay the price. The elder one, a fair-haired blue-eyed boy of twelve, was proclaimed as Edward V but he was never crowned. He had not been king three months, when he and his brother were sent by their uncle Richard to live in the Tower. They were never seen alive again, but years afterwards their bones were found buried under a staircase.

Meanwhile Uncle Richard had himself crowned with every pomp. Was he the murderer of his nephews? That is a mystery, but most people think he was. We can be sure that as he walked to the abbey under the canopy of purple silk, there were suspicious looks and doubtful glances from the crowd who jostled, as London crowds have always done, to see a king. And as he sat in state upon the throne, his dark eyes must have searched the faces of the nobles as they knelt and swore their homage, wondering how many meant to keep that solemn oath.

In three short years he was to know the worst. In 1485 Henry Tudor landed at Milford Haven and claimed the crown of England, through his mother, a daughter of the House of Lancaster. Galloping horses carried the news from castle to castle, and barons put on armour, and called out their men to fight once again for York or Lancaster.

Shakespeare has painted Richard as a coward, calling for a horse to flee from his great battle, Bosworth Field. But whatever his faults the courage of the Plantagenets was strong in him. When in the shock of battle he saw his men desert him, he charged again and again at the head of his dwindling force, a golden crown on his helmet and his sword flashing about it defending it to the last. Almost alone he fought his way to where Henry's standard flew, cut down the standard-bearer, and fell "borne down by numbers" at his rival's feet. The crown rolled from his head, and later that day one of the nobles picked it out of a hawthorn bush and set it on the head of Henry Tudor.

Chapter VII

THE WELSH HEIRS OF ENGLAND

A<small>S HENRY TUDOR</small> rode in triumph towards London, the citizens made ready to welcome yet another warrior king, and bring out banners to decorate the streets as they had done in turn for Lancaster and York. To their surprise Henry entered his capital not as a soldier but "in a covered chariot, a mode of travelling never before used except by females". It was a sign of the changing times. The reign of barbarism was over. The new king had fought his first and last battle, and was going to devote himself to crushing the strength of the barons, so that warfare could not be their pastime any more.

Elizabeth, "the White Rose of York", sister of the little king who perished in the tower, might have been a rival for his throne, but Henry settled that problem by marrying her. The old feud was ended, and the red and white rose, combined together, became the badge of the House of Tudor.

England rejoiced to have peace, and a king and queen, both of royal descent, who had never murdered anyone. Elizabeth was beautiful and virtuous; Henry was a stern man but just and capable, and very careful with money. (It was high time too that someone was.) For his coronation no expense was spared, but it was all noted down to the last penny. Henry seems to have had a complete trousseau, for besides his official robes, half a dozen long gowns, and as many doublets, cloaks, surcoats and "jakettes" are mentioned in the accounts. They sound very splendid: "a longe mantelle with a trayne of crimsin saten furred with menever" (twenty-two yards of satin were allowed for this, and George, the King's Tailor, got £1 for making it), "a longe gowne of purpul cloth of gold", "a jakette of blake velvet furred with bogey"—and so forth. We read of velvet trapping for the horses, embroidered with Welsh dragons and Tudor roses, of green and white satin and "hostriche feders" for the henchmen, and at least five hundred yards of red cloth for one thing and another. But among these expensive items nothing has been forgotten, "$\frac{1}{2}$ lb red thread price 8d", "item a bagge 5d", "for inke 2d". A careful eye was checking every penny.

After this extravagance Henry settled down to a more quiet life, and no doubt wore his fine clothes for the rest of his reign. Soon Englishmen were glad to see a family growing up, for what they feared most was another disputed succession. The eldest boy was called Arthur after the King of the Round Table (for Henry loved the legends and romances of his native Wales). But it seems to have been an unlucky name for heirs to the English throne. Like that other Arthur whom John had murdered, Arthur Tudor never became king. He died at Ludlow at the age of sixteen, and his brother Henry succeeded in his stead.

Henry VIII is familiar to us all with his burly figure and twinkling eyes. For fine clothes and the pomp of majesty he outshone all the kings who had gone before him, and his power was so great that he was able to defy the Pope, and to make himself supreme head of the Church of England. Only a year or so before the Pope had given him the title of Defender of the Faith because he was such a pious member of the Catholic Church. Now he led the movement away from it, because he found it suited his private affairs—but he kept the title and his heirs have borne it ever since.

It was a wonderful reign for outward show. There was always something to be seen in London, for the king moved here and there, from the old palace at Westminster to his new country house St James's, or by river in a gilded barge to Greenwich or Richmond or Hampton Court. As for coronations there were no less than five in the one reign. For he married six times and all but one of his wives were crowned with brilliant pageantry. The more gloomy scenes of divorces and executions came in between.

One of the reasons he married so often was his anxiety for the succession. As he had no brothers it was most important for him to have sons. But in spite of all his marriages he died leaving only one sickly son and two daughters. Strangely contrasting were those three, each the child of a different mother. First Mary, daughter of the old king's first wife, Katherine of Aragon, half Spanish, dark and passionate, and embittered because her mother had been treated so badly; then Elizabeth, a red-haired girl whose mother, pretty Anne Boleyn, had lost her head on the scaffold. No one knew much about her. Lastly the heir, Edward, a fragile boy of nine, clever at his books but consumptive. He was crowned as Edward VI, but the nobles, guessing he had not long to live, were already eyeing his sisters and his cousins and laying their plans.

There had never been a queen of England, but it was clear that there was going to be one now, for every other member of the royal family was a woman, and it was by no means sure which of them was the heir. Mary Tudor had the best claim, but when Henry VIII was angry with her mother he had debarred her from the succession, and

Lady Jane Grey

later had done the same by Elizabeth. This made it possible for men to argue that the real heir was Mary Queen of Scots, the granddaughter of Henry's elder sister; or, if a Protestant was to be preferred, Lady Jane Grey, the granddaughter of his younger sister. Of these four young women so near to the throne, all were to bear the name of queen, and two were to lose their heads; but in 1550 no one could have guessed which.

As poor little Edward lay dying, the nobles were rushing to support different princesses. One of them tried to marry Elizabeth, and was executed for his impertinence. Another succeeded in marrying Jane, who was as harmless as she was good and pretty. No sooner was Edward dead than Jane's relatives tried to make her queen.

Mary Tudor was on her way to London, knowing nothing of all this, but a loyal messenger met her in the High Street of Hoddesdon, and broke the news that her brother was dead and treason afoot towards herself. Murmuring a prayer, Mary turned her horse's head northwards again and, followed by her little party of attendants, galloped off into the dusk.

Framlingham Castle in Suffolk first flew the standard of a Queen of England. There Mary and her ladies set up their court, while the local gentry hastened to offer their support. From day to day their strength grew, as armed knights and their men gathered to fight for the eldest daughter of old King Harry. At last London declared for her; poor little Jane was clapped into the Tower, where she was afterwards executed, and the citizens turned out to welcome "Madame Mary, Queen of England".

Then came the problem of how to crown her, but the conclusion that all the great men of Church and State came to was that even if the monarch were a woman, not one jot of the ceremonial could be altered.

The solemnity began when Mary went by water to the Tower and knighted a number of gentlemen. The next day she went in procession to Westminster, carried in a litter between six white horses. Behind her rode seventy ladies on horseback, all in crimson velvet. The Princess Elizabeth had a place of honour, and all the nobles of England were there.

The old palace of Westminster had lately been burnt, little besides the great hall remaining, so Mary did not sleep there as sovereigns had always done on the eve of their coronations, but at Whitehall Palace, a little farther down the river. In the morning her barge brought her to Westminster Hall, where the ceremonies began. Later, in the Abbey, she was anointed by the Archbishop of York (Canterbury being in prison). The sword was girded on, the great spurs fixed to her feet, and so she was crowned "in all particulars like unto a king".

Her reign was a tragedy. An ardent Roman Catholic, she thought it her duty to force England to submit to the Pope again, and to burn those who would not agree with her. She married the hated King of Spain, and, if she had borne a son, he would have been three-quarters Spanish. It was a terrible danger, but it passed away when Mary died childless and broken-hearted.

Queen Elizabeth bears one of the most famous names in history. But in 1558 no one knew very much of the young woman of twenty-five, who came riding to London from her house at Hatfield one fine autumn day. But all the same "men did eat and make merry because of the new queen", for she had her father's red hair and merry eyes, and she was English through and through. There was little money in the treasury for coronation expenses, and what was more there was hardly a bishop to be found to crown her. The Archbishop of Canterbury was dead, and so great had been the religious upheaval that all the other bishops were burnt, or in prison, or would have preferred Scottish Mary as queen. At the last moment the Bishop of Carlisle was persuaded to crown Elizabeth, and as it was too late to send for his robes he borrowed those of the Bishop of London.

In spite of these difficulties London was determined to give their English queen a rousing welcome. The mercers and haberdashers, the grocers and all the other honourable companies of tradesmen, put their heads together to think of new decorations and entertainments, and when the procession issued from the Tower, the high timber houses of Old London were ablaze with banners, cloths and tapestries. Never was loyalty more graciously received than by the new queen. Again and again the royal chariot was stopped, so that she might see the shows prepared for her, and receive from poor women posies of wild flowers and rosemary. An arch had been erected over Gracechurch Street, bearing above it figures of Elizabeth's parents and grandparents in a bower of red and white roses, with a figure of the queen herself perched on top like Jack on the Beanstalk. In Cheapside eight children recited moral verses, and, farther on, Time and Truth presented her with a bible. An acrobat performed tricks on the cross of St Paul's, and a couple of giants bowed down to her at Temple Bar.

So Elizabeth came to Whitehall, and the next day (18 July) was crowned queen. At the banquet that followed, Sir Edward Dymoke, riding in as champion, proclaimed her styles, and challenged the world to deny her right as "the most high and mighty princess, our dread Sovereign, Lady Elizabeth by the grace of God, Queen of England, France and Ireland, Defender of the Faith"—so much was according to custom, but he added

The Crowning of Queen Elizabeth

unexpectedly—"most worthy Empress from the Orkney Islands to the Mountains Pyrenee". It sounded well to claim Scotland as well as France, but the young Queen of Scots, far from submitting to Elizabeth, was at that very time styling herself Queen of England.

There is no need to tell of the greatness of Elizabeth; how the great lords served her humbly, and Parliament trembled when she stamped her foot; how men adventured and fought for her and poets sang of her; how half the princes in Europe sought her in marriage and she would have none of them; and how under her single rule England grew strong and rich.

She was English; she was King Harry's daughter, but her mother came from the people, from the family of a plain citizen of London. In peaceful years she loved to visit her nobles in their fine new country houses, riding through town and country with a fine company of lords and ladies. Everywhere she went her subjects, rich and poor, flocked to see her, and treasured the memory of her visits.

When war broke out with Spain, she was ready to lead the English armies, for she was as fierce as her father. When her beautiful but unfortunate cousin, Mary of Scotland, fell into her hands, Elizabeth kept her a prisoner for twenty years, and finally had her executed, an act of cruelty which can never be forgotten. But it was Mary who triumphed in the end, for the House of Tudor ended with Elizabeth. It was Mary's son who succeeded her, and Mary's descendant is on the throne today.

Chapter VIII

THE SCOTTISH HEIRS OF ENGLAND

N a dark night in the spring of 1603 a horseman galloped through the muddy lanes of England, bearing news that was to mark a new age in our history. Northwards he rode, on and on, until at last, weary and mudstained, he clattered over the cobbles of Edinburgh and into the courtyard of Holyrood Palace. James VI, King of Scotland, was going to bed, but hearing the messenger he came out in his nightshirt, and it was thus that he received the news that Elizabeth was dead, and he King of England.

Centuries before, the mighty Edwards had tried to conquer Scotland and had failed. Now fate had done what armies could not do. If Henry VIII had had a single grandchild, Scotland might have remained a separate country, but his three children had died childless and so it was the grandson of his sister who sat upon his throne. James was descended from Robert Bruce and from the ancient Stewart kings. He could not remember his unhappy beautiful mother and did not take after her in the least. The only romantic thing he ever did was to rescue his queen when she was wrecked on the coast of Norway on her way to Scotland. Her ships were ice-bound in a desolate region, and James abandoned his kingdom and set out in a small ship through ice and snow and brought her safely to Scotland. After that he settled down and never did anything daring again.

So James rode royally to London and was crowned King of England on the old stone that had been stolen from his ancestors. And Englishmen accepted him gladly, because anything seemed better than a war about the crown.

If James was a dull king, his court was brilliant. The time was gone when the nobles cared only for fighting. Now they had learned to enjoy poetry and the arts. There was good music and witty conversation to be heard in Whitehall Palace, and fine pictures on its walls, while its amusements were provided by Ben Jonson and Will Shakespeare.

James called his two kingdoms Great Britain, a high-sounding name which has served well ever since, and he quartered his standard again, having lions and lilies in two quarters, the red lion of Scotland in the third and the harp of Ireland in the fourth quarter.

An unhappy fate has several times fallen on the eldest sons of our kings. Now again the heir to the throne, the beloved Henry, Prince of Wales, died young, so that James was succeeded by his second son Charles.

His handsome looks, his long brown curls and dreamy eyes, his gentle courtesy and princely dignity, and above all his sincere desire to serve God, made Charles I a king whom Englishmen and Scotsmen alike could love and honour. But although a virtuous man, he was not a clever statesman. Old quarrels not of his making burst over his head, and because he held to his own beliefs and would not give way to the storm he lost his kingdom and his life.

"Be thou faithful unto death, and I will give thee a crown of life." That was the text of the sermon preached at Charles's coronation. In later days men remembered it with awe. To Charles the service meant more than to most kings. He believed most devoutly that it gave him a real sanctity, raising him so high above all other men that his word must always be their law. But the power of Parliament was growing and Englishmen were no longer willing to submit to the king's will as they had done in the days of King Henry VIII. Since Charles would not give up the authority which, as he believed, had been given him by God, the kingdom was rent again by civil war. Englishmen had to decide whether they would fight for king or Parliament. The king was fighting for an old idea—and there were many who stood by him loyally—Parliament for a new one which was to conquer in the end.

It was a terrible time, for families were divided, and brothers killed each other in English fields. Other causes were involved besides the power of the king, for the Puritans in Parliament wished to do away with the authority of the bishops and to abolish the Prayer Book. Charles took his duties, as supreme governor of the Church of England, seriously, and was prepared to die for the Church. When he was a prisoner in the hands of his enemies he might have consented to give up his power over the State, but he would not give up his Church. So, on a bitter morning, 30 January 1649, he walked between Roundhead soldiers, from St James's Palace to Whitehall, where a scaffold had been erected. With simple dignity he mounted it, prayed a while, and then with one last word, "Remember", "bowed his comely head" upon the block. The axe flashed and a deep groan rose from the crowd, for Charles the King was now Charles the Martyr.

Oliver Cromwell was now master of Parliament and his army was master of England. He took the old regalia from the abbey, and gave orders that it should be utterly destroyed. He sold the gold and the jewels for what their mere weight was worth.

The crown of St Edward, with which every sovereign had been crowned for six hundred years, was valued at £1110, being covered with jewels; but that of Edith, St Edward's queen, fetched only £16. The "great golden spurs", which it had long been the proud right of the Earls of Pembroke to carry in procession, went for £1. 13s. 4d., and most horrible of all, the crown of

Alfred, which we should now hold as priceless, was melted down for £248. 10s. The most pathetic part of the list comes last:

"One crimson taffety robe, very old, valued at 10/-.

"One liver coloured silk robe, very old and worth nothing.

"One pair of buskins, cloth of silver and silver stockins, very old, valued at 2/6.

"One pair of gloves embroidered with gold at 1/-.

"One old comb of bone worth nothing."

These were the robes of the regalia reverently put upon each king after his anointing—so old indeed that they were believed to be the same robes that had been used since Saxon times. The old comb had arranged St Edward's hair.

Then Cromwell turned his attention to the Scots who were still loyal to their old royal family, and who now

hailed young Charles, Prince of Wales, as their king.
With fire and sword he broke down their resistance, but
in one thing he was defeated. The Scottish regalia which
he hoped to destroy, as he had destroyed the royal
emblems of England, were in Edinburgh Castle. But
when after a long siege the castle fell to him, nothing or
the sort could be found. During the siege it had all been
smuggled out with the aid of a minister's wife from the
town, a respectable woman, who had been allowed to go
in to see a sick friend. When she returned, Cromwell's
soldiers had allowed her to pass through their lines on
her old nag, never guessing that the distaff which she
carried, all twisted round with wool, was the sceptre of
Scotland; and that tucked away under her ample skirts
was the crown of Robert Bruce. So these treasures were
saved and may still be seen in Edinburgh Castle.

Meanwhile the Scots had crowned Charles II in their
ancient royal church of Scone. But Cromwell's Round-
heads defeated his army so completely that he was forced
to fly for his life. A thousand pounds was offered for his
capture. Although many must have recognized the tall
dark young man "above two yards high", no one was
base enough to betray him. For six weeks he dodged
about the country, disguised as a woman, or as a servant,
helped by many loyal subjects and hunted by Cromwell's
soldiers. It is well known how once he hid in an oak,

> While underneath the Roundheads rode
> And hummed a surly hymn.

That was only one of many adventures, before at last

he got safely aboard a ship sailing from Shoreham. One by one the children of Charles I reached France in safety, all except one little princess, Elizabeth, who died in captivity in Carisbrooke Castle. The second son, James, Duke of York, escaped from St James's Palace during a skilful game of hide and seek, and boarded a fishing smack in the clothes of a serving maid. The youngest of the family, little Henrietta, was smuggled out of the country, when only two years old, disguised in rags and dirt as a pedlar's child. With their widowed mother, Queen Henrietta Maria, they settled down in exiled poverty, to wait the next turn of fortune's wheel.

Once Cromwell had established his power Englishmen submitted to it more or less peaceably, but no sooner was he dead than a thrill ran through the nation as if it were awaking from a bad dream. England had tried the experiment of having no king and proved that she did not like it. At first the name of Charles II was only whispered, but soon men found that they were all of the same mind. The army was for him; Parliament was for him; the people were for him, and when, on 18 May 1660, the heralds proclaimed him at Westminster, the shout that went up drowned the pealing of the bells.

On 25 May he landed at Dover and the white cliffs were black with loyal subjects cheering themselves hoarse as his ship, the *Naseby*, drew in to the shore. On the 29th, his thirtieth birthday, he entered London "with a triumph of above twenty thousand horse and foot, brandishing their swords and shouting with inexpressible joy, the ways strewed with flowers, the bells ringing, the

Welcoming King Charles

streets hung with tapestry, fountains running with wine". Long into the night singing and dancing continued in the streets, and from end to end of England bonfires blazed in every village. It was a real expression of deep feeling long pent up and bursting out now in such a frenzy of joy, that seldom in our history has anything equalled it. The nearest thing to it that any of us has seen was the Jubilee of George V. On both occasions the brilliance of the procession was outshone by the enthusiasm of the crowd. In 1935 it was love of the man himself that inspired it. In 1660 it was the monarchy.

They were gay months that followed and preparations went forward busily for the coronation. Charles ordered the Master of the Jewel House to prepare a complete new set of regalia, the various articles to be exact copies of those that had been destroyed, and like them to be called St Edward's. The original gold was gone for ever, but any of the old jewels that could be traced were bought back and reset in the new crowns. The Master of the King's Wardrobe had to provide the robes for the great day—the shirt with the openings for anointing, the overshirt of scarlet, the long tunic and embroidered pall and all the priestly and knightly ornaments to be put on before the altar.

All but the robes are still in use. They are kept in the Tower with the other crown jewels except when wanted for state occasions. Among them is the original eagle-shaped ampulla which was found unbroken at the Restoration, and which will be used to anoint George VI. But new robes are made for each new king, for it has become the custom for kings to be buried in their coronation clothes. The long tunics and rich palls, embroidered with lilies, roses, shamrocks and thistles, lie with their royal owners in the grave.

Charles rode through London before his coronation, with such magnificence "as no age hath seen the like in this or any other kingdom". The Horse Guards were much admired for their splendid mounts and scarlet plumes. The next day all London did its best to pack into the abbey. Master Pepys, who kept a diary, was there, and squeezed into the banqueting hall too. He managed to get hold of four rabbits and a pullet from one of the lower tables, and was much contented with the whole affair. So were all Englishmen, for they had a king again.

Chapter IX

CROWN AND CONSTITUTION

HE restoration is like the end of a fairy story, and one would like to add that "they lived happy ever after". But the misfortunes of the House of Stewart were not nearly over. Charles II indeed managed to keep his throne and reigned merrily till the end of his life, largely because of his own good sense; for he forgave his enemies and tried to please everyone. But his brother James, who succeeded him, was a singularly tactless person. He made enemies as easily as Charles had made friends and, from the moment he came to the throne, things went wrong.

To begin with he disappointed the Londoners by having no procession from the Tower. London was growing and already the congestion in the narrow streets was terrible. Many directions had been issued for Charles II's procession to prevent disorder, for instance "that no person whatsoever doe that day ride upon any unruly or striking horse". These were the forerunners of the elaborate traffic regulations of today. In James II's time the procession seemed too difficult and expensive and was abandoned for ever. This was a small thing compared to the troubles that were coming, but in coronation ceremonies superstitious people were always quick to see omens of the new reign. Any change seemed an unlucky sign. And when during the service the crown fitted so badly that it nearly fell off, men shook their heads gloomily.

The old quarrels over Church and Parliament were not yet over. Some things were settled, for instance that Englishmen wanted a king, and would not try to do without one again, but they wanted the monarchy to be very different from what it had been. They wanted it to be "constitutional" and that was a new idea. It meant that the king had his appointed place in the constitution and must keep to it. He was to be something like the captain of a football team, who has great influence in holding his side together and directing their play, but must himself be bound by the rules of the game as much as anyone. Because James had the old idea that the king could make or break rules to suit himself, he soon got into trouble.

The religious question was settled, too; the Church of England, for which Charles I had died, was firmly established in the hearts of the people. But James was a Roman Catholic. Englishmen at that time were stupidly bitter about Papists (as they called them) and even afraid of them, for old men's grandfathers could remember the burning of Protestants in Catholic Mary's day. When James began favouring Catholics there was a panic, and as he would never give way in anything, he soon found himself opposed to yet another strong current of feeling.

He had married Anne Hyde, daughter of an English earl. She died before he came to the throne, leaving two daughters, Mary and Anne, stout, sensible Protestant princesses. They were not romantic, but people looked forward to the day when one of them should come to the throne and behave more reasonably than her father. James's second wife was Mary of Modena, a young Catholic princess from Italy; and when she presented him with a baby son, instead of rejoicings at an heir to the throne, there was open discontent. It seemed clear that the prince would be brought up as a Catholic and reign instead of Protestant Mary.

This unfortunate little prince came into the world just when the feeling against his father was swelling into a great tide and, before the baby was six months old, James, a sick man, gave way before it. Seeing that all men were against him, he resolved to escape from the country. His first anxiety was for the safety of his wife and his son; and, on a dark winter night, the young queen stole down a secret stairway out of Whitehall Palace, with her baby in her arms. One lady-in-waiting followed with a bundle of clothes and jewels (including St Edward's sapphire), and two loyal gentlemen completed the little party. A rowing boat was waiting at the steps and they set out across the black and choppy water of the Thames, with snow falling heavily upon them. Once across, the gentlemen ran to find the coach which was expected, while the queen with her baby huddled against the wall of old Lambeth church, in cold and darkness. The coach came at last; a yacht was waiting at Gravesend; and the heir of the Stewart kings left England, never to see it again. A few days later James II joined them in France, while in London bells were ringing for his daughter Mary, and her Dutch husband William.

The long struggle between Crown and Parliament was over, and Parliament had won. An Act was passed stating that no king might ever again overrule the laws of the land, and that no Roman Catholic could ever be king. That ruled out James and his son, and made Mary the rightful heir. As her husband was also descended from Charles I, and was a strong-minded man, who refused to be his "own wife's gentleman usher", they were proclaimed as joint sovereigns reigning together. Mary's sister Anne was the next heir and, if neither of them left any children, the succession was to pass to a distant cousin, the Duchess of Hanover, who was the nearest member of the royal family to be a Protestant.

Many of the people who had sworn homage to James II denied that Parliament had the right to alter the succession. Some went willingly into exile with him, not because they admired him, but because they would not break their oath of loyalty. Others were content to submit to William and Mary, though they secretly drank to "the King over the water". But the principle which Parliament had now asserted, that kings can only reign by the consent of their people, is a very ancient one. Saxon kings had to be chosen by the "Witan"; and a necessary part of the coronation has always been the voice of the people giving their consent, after the Recognition.

All the important developments in our monarchy have been represented in the coronation, so now we find that for William and Mary the service was revised. It is very remarkable that all through the religious changes of the last century it had never been altered at all, except that in James I's reign it had been translated from Latin into English. All the monarchs, whether Protestant or Catholic, had taken the old Oath to maintain the Church as it was in the time of Edward the Confessor. This had come to be sheer nonsense and was now replaced by the promise which the king still makes, to maintain "the Protestant reformed religion as established by law". One addition was made to the regalia, a bible, which was presented after the crowning.

In one respect this coronation was unique. There have never been before or since a king and queen reigning, both as sovereigns. The queen was not crowned after the king with a simpler ceremony. King and queen sat side by side on two thrones of equal height. A second crown had been provided so that they could be crowned together, and they took the Oath in chorus.

William and Mary were not picturesque, and Anne, who followed them, was a colourless though well-meaning woman. Though England grew prosperous in her day she had little to do with it. The most important event in her reign was her death. All her children had died before her, and England was alive with rumours, that James II's son was coming to claim his own. So he might have done, and won it too, if he had been quick and bold, for old loyalties still ran strong, but he dallied, and the chance was lost for ever. George of Hanover, the heir supported by Parliament, was ready to mount the throne. He was the grandson of James I's daughter (for whose wedding Shakespeare had written his last play), but he was a stodgy German speaking not a word of English. Yet the nation accepted him, for the sake of peace.

Four Georges followed each other in succession, covering a hundred years in all. They are momentous years in the history of England but not in the history of kings. Parliament was master and the power of the crown sank almost to nothing. But, although Englishmen had given their loyalty rather grudgingly to the new royal line, they did not easily withdraw it. That was proved in 1745, when James II's grandson, Prince Charles Edward, landed on a tiny island off the Scottish coast, to claim the inheritance of his forefathers. The Highlands rose for him, but England stood by George II. On the night the news reached London that Bonnie Prince Charlie had won a great victory at Prestonpans, and was about to invade England, the king was to attend a musical performance at Drury Lane. The management hastily added a suitable song to the programme. It was set to an old tune and the words consisted mostly of the repetition of a time-honoured expression of loyalty. It was "God Save the King", which has since become the national anthem. The second verse, which is seldom sung now, about "scattering his enemies", referred to Prince Charlie and his highlanders. That romantic young man marched bravely into England, and wearily out again. Many people drank a health to him, but few would give up peace and security for his sake. At last he found

Wellington and the King's Champion

himself, like his great-uncle Charles II, a hunted outlaw, hiding in caves and woods in many disguises until at last he escaped—to die in Rome, years later, a childless, crabbed old man. His only brother was a cardinal of the Roman Catholic Church, and with him the direct male line of the House of Stewart ended.' Before he died he gave back to George III the sapphire of St Edward, which had been carried off by the exiled Stewarts. It is now set in the cross, surmounting the crown. The old feud is ended.

George III was a real Englishman at last. He loved the countryside and quiet family life. He had fifteen sons and daughters and reigned for fifty-nine years respected by all his subjects. Under him the dignity of the crown revived a little; but with his son George IV it sank lower than ever. A fashionable fop, he thought of little but his elegant appearance (until he grew enormously fat). To him the ancient ceremony of coronation was an opportunity for dressing-up, rather than a solemn service.

The coronation banquet then took place for the last time. The Duke of Wellington, as Lord High Constable, ushered in the dishes, on horseback. The Archbishop of Canterbury, as Lord of the Manor of Addington, had the right of presenting the dish of "dilligrout", which a deputy performed for him. The Champion (Henry Dymoke) was more magnificent than any of his ancestors, with enormous plumes of feathers on his helmet. Everything was as splendid as could be, but it was more like playing at charades, than any real honour to a king. Serious-minded people were disgusted and, like the procession through the city, the banquet was given up. Only the service of coronation remains as our legacy from the past.

Again the heir to the throne, Princess Charlotte, died, and George IV's brother, William, a good-tempered sailor, reigned for seven years. His heir was his niece, the Princess Victoria. In the small hours of 20 June 1837 William IV died and horsemen galloped to Kensington Palace to rouse that princess from her bed, and to tell her she was Queen of England.

Chapter X

CROWN AND EMPIRE

IT was just a hundred years ago that eighteen-year-old Victoria stood in her dressing gown, with tears in her eyes, resolving to be worthy of her high calling. It was a resolve in which she never failed. Some people laugh at this great queen and look down on the Victorian age. That is just the stupid habit people have always had of thinking themselves superior to the generation before them. No doubt in Stewart times people scoffed at the Elizabethans, just as our grandchildren will scoff at us.

In the two hundred years before Victoria's accession the monarchy had lost its old power. In the hundred years since then it has found a new one. Our kings now do not rule; they guide and influence the nation in a way that fits in with the law of the land. They do not struggle against Parliament; they give it their authority and advice. They are above all politics and, whatever party is in power, the king's support is always behind it, giving strength and continuity.

This change had not come easily. One king had lost his head, and another his crown, before it was accomplished. When Victoria came to the throne, the monarchy had even lost its dignity. Sixty-four years later when she died, after the longest reign in our history, such a halo of majesty and mystery surrounded her, that one has to go back to the first beginnings of our race to equal it, when the primitive tribes reverenced their kings as being akin to gods.

The queen herself from the moment she came to the throne was as much aware of her dignity as anyone, and liked to be treated with proper respect—but she was also a very genuine and sincere person, and unlike her late uncle George hated anything theatrical. On points of ceremonial her word was law, and she soon showed her character by insisting that the Coronation Service should be simplified. To her it was a solemn "hallowing", not a mere pageant for the crowds, and each ceremony had a deep inward meaning. Details which had lost their significance were left out.

Three years later she married a German prince, Albert of Saxe-Coburg-Gotha, and they had a fine family, nine children, all of whom grew up beloved and honoured. Three of them are still living. They married into nearly all the royal families of Europe, and seven of Victoria's grandchildren became kings or queens. Royalties often arrived in England in those days, to pay their respects, at Windsor, to the First Lady in the world. The little lady in her shawl and bustle and widow's cap, whose advice swayed the greatest politicians of a great age, had more influence over her country than there is room in this book to tell.

The queen was so devoted to her husband that not only her sons, but all her grandsons and great-grandsons, born in her lifetime, were given Albert as one of their

names. After he died she lived a very retired life, making few public appearances. One of them will be always remembered—her Diamond Jubilee, when London was packed with loyal crowds cheering wildly and straining to see the little withered old lady, sitting so upright in her carriage. She lived to see three generations of heirs to her crown, and was able to advise her grandson George on the upbringing of his sons. Little Edward and Albert had already gone into sailor suits when she died.

The wonderful reign ended at last, and the nation felt lost and bewildered without a queen.

Edward VII had been Prince of Wales for nearly sixty years. He was king for only nine. He upheld the high dignity of the crown and passed it on to his son George, as honoured as when he had received it.

When George V became king

many people thought him rather dull, but time was to prove them very wrong. At the end of the Great War, when kingdoms were falling to pieces, and crowns trampled under the feet of revolution, he raised the honour of the crown of England higher than it had ever been before and made it the envy of the world.

This quiet unassuming man had travelled more widely in his empire than any king before him, and showed an instinctive understanding of his many peoples. Early in his reign he delighted his Indian subjects by going in person with Queen Mary to Delhi to be crowned Emperor of India, and to receive the homage of its ruling Princes amid scenes of dazzling splendour.

The rejoicings at his Jubilee, in the last year of his life, not only touched his heart but surprised him for, being the most modest of men, he had always thought himself "a very ordinary sort of fellow". But courage, and simplicity, and honesty are not qualities to be despised, and in the long procession of our kings we must look right back to Alfred the Great to find his equal.

It is not only the love of the people that has given the crown a new power. In the last century, men and women from Great Britain have gone to the ends of the earth and have peopled new lands. At first they formed an Empire in the true sense of the word, because they were ruled by the Government of England; but now four of these new countries, Canada, Australia, South Africa and New Zealand, govern themselves and form with Great Britain a Commonwealth of free nations. They are bound together by language and tradition, but there is no legal bond between them except their loyalty to the king. In the tropical colonies and in India, many nations, with different languages and faiths, hail the King as their Emperor. Once it would have seemed impossible for one man to hold the loyalty of four hundred million people scattered over the globe—but new marvels in this amazing age have helped to make it possible. Photography has made the face of the king familiar to his remotest subjects; by wireless the news of his doings flashes instantaneously across the oceans; and, most wonderful of all, his voice can speak to all his people, black, brown or white, on mountain or prairie or coral island. In this way George V became known to his people in a new and personal way, and earned a tribute of love and loyalty, such as no monarch has ever had before.

His eldest son, Edward VIII, renounced that inheritance. A clash came between his father's high ideals of kingship and his own wishes. He disappointed the millions of people whose hopes were set on him, and he has passed on the crown to his brother.

Albert of York, a second son, like his father whose name he has chosen to take, is also like him a sailor. He has been through the hard discipline of a naval life and served in action at the Battle of Jutland. Like his father again, he retired from the sea to devote himself to public duties and to the happy cares of a family. There is every reason to believe that he will be like him also in those qualities of quiet steadiness and devotion to duty which gave his father the name of George the Beloved.

There have been two coronations in this century—that of Edward VII and his queen, Alexandra of Denmark, who was so beautiful that, though she was a grandmother at the time, a witness described her as "a lovely vision from fairyland"; then that of their son George V with Mary of Teck, an English-born princess, whom we still have with us to be loved and honoured.

Now there is to be a third, that of George VI and Elizabeth, first Scottish Queen since the Union. Once again the old ceremonies are performed—the trumpets blow, the banners float in the air and the heralds proclaim: "George VI, by the Grace of God, of Great Britain, Ireland and the Dominions beyond the Sea, King, Defender of the Faith, Emperor of India."

Some of the old customs are changed but the service itself remains—the same rite that hallowed the warlike Plantagenets, the powerful Tudors, and the unhappy Stewarts—an expression of the new devotion to the crown, inspired by Victoria and strengthened by her son and grandson. The voice of the people and the vow of the king are full of real meaning. The oil that gives sanctity, the sword to be used for God, the sceptre of justice and mercy, the spurs of knighthood and the robes of the priest, all signify the dedication of the king to God as the representative of his people.

The ancient words are still spoken, "God crown you with a crown of Glory and Righteousness"; and as the archbishop sets the jewelled emblem on the king's head, the trumpets sound, the people shout, guns outside take

King George VI and Queen Elizabeth

up the roar, and in a flash of velvet and gold all the peers of England put on their coronets.

Then princes and bishops and peers of the land kneel before their new king, taking off their coronets in token of humility. The senior one of each rank says on behalf of the others the old words, that have come down to us from the Middle Ages: "I (*name*) do become your liegeman of life and limb and of earthly worship, and faith and truth I bear unto you to live and die against all manner of folk. So help me God."

Then the queen is crowned, and again trumpets and guns announce it to the world. The peeresses put on their coronets, and the queen returning to her throne beside the king, curtseys to him, for she too is his subject.

In this modern world the news that the king and queen are crowned will resound not only through London, but will echo right across the world. Four hundred million people will join in the shout: "God save King George VI and Queen Elizabeth."